I0815581

A Day in the Life of an Ant

Julie Murray

Abdo Kids Junior
is an Imprint of Abdo Kids
abdobooks.com

Abdo
A DAY IN THE LIFE
OF AN ANIMAL
Kids

abdobooks.com

Published by Abdo Kids, a division of ABDO, P.O. Box 398166, Minneapolis, Minnesota 55439.

Printed in the United States of America, North Mankato, Minnesota.

102025

012026

Photo Credits: AdobeStock, Alamy, Shutterstock

Production Contributors: Teddy Borth, Jennie Forsberg, Grace Hansen

Design Contributors: Candice Keimig, Pakou Moua

Library of Congress Control Number: 2025936506

Publisher's Cataloging-in-Publication Data

Names: Murray, Julie, author.

Title: A day in the life of an Ant / by Julie Murray

Description: Minneapolis, Minnesota : Abdo Kids, 2026 | Series: A day in the life of an animal | Includes online resources and index.

Identifiers: ISBN 9798384907336 (lib. bdg.) | ISBN 9798384908036 (ebook) | ISBN 9798384908388 (read-to-me ebook)

Subjects: LCSH: Ants--Juvenile literature. | Ants--Behavior--Juvenile literature. | Insects--Juvenile literature. | Insects--Behavior--Juvenile literature. | Animal behavior--Juvenile literature. | Entomology--Juvenile literature.

Classification: DDC 595.796--dc23

Table of Contents

An Ant's Day

The sun is rising.

The ant **colony** comes to life!

Ants work as a team.

Each ant has a job to do.

They search for food.

They carry it back to the nest.

They take care of the **queen** and her eggs.

Queen
Egg

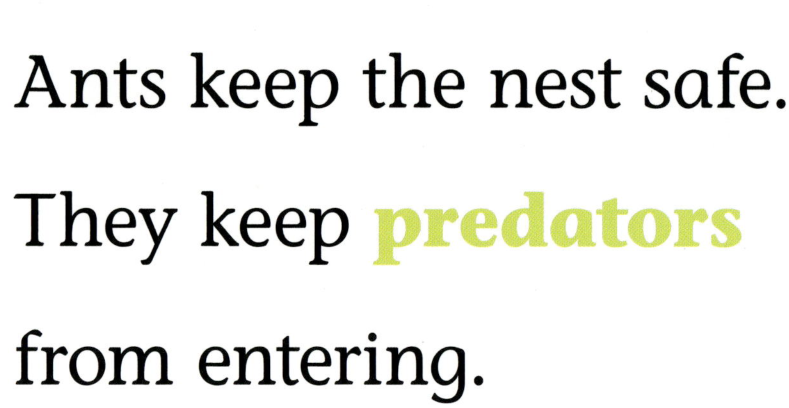

Ants keep the nest safe. They keep **predators** from entering.

They take short naps.

They take turns resting.

Ants care for the nest.

Some build new tunnels.

Inside an ant nest

The sun goes down.

Most ants go back to the nest.

Their work never stops.

The **colony** is always busy!

Ant Facts

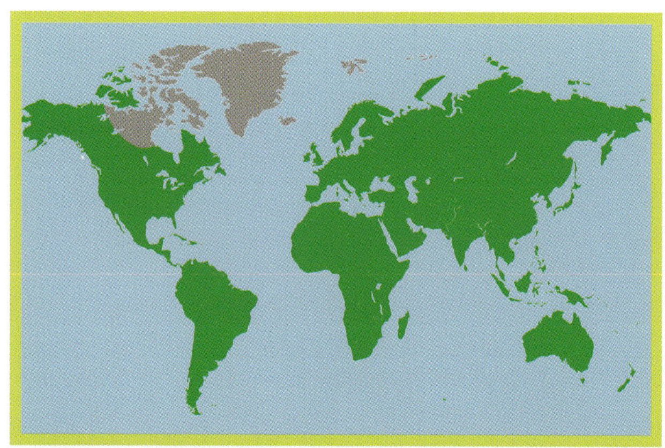

Ants live on every continent except Antarctica

A **queen** ant can live around 15 years

Male ants usually live just 2 weeks

Worker ants (females) live for about 7 years

Glossary

colony

a group of animals of the same type living closely together.

predator

an animal that hunts other animals for food.

queen

the adult female in an ant colony that lays eggs. She is usually the mother of all other ants in that colony.

Index

Visit **abdokids.com** to access crafts, games, videos, and more!